# Table of Contents



I0786900

# Racing to Win

Racers speed their dirt bikes along a dirt course. They take tight turns, bounce on hills, and fly high on jumps.

Racing toward the finish line, each rider wants to be the first to cross. Then they will win the Motocross race.

Riders cross the finish line of the FIM Motocross World Championship.

# More about Motocross

Motocross is a dirt bike racing competition. Riders race on human-made or natural courses. Races are held inside or outside.

Courses have hills, turns, and muddy areas. They are between 1 and 3 miles (1.6 to 4.8 km) long. Races are fast, lasting about 40 minutes or less.

Bikes and riders can get covered in mud and dirt during a race.

A person repairing their bike

Motocross competitions are split into two heats, or motos. Each heat is a race around the track. Riders can get their bike fixed between heats.

Riders earn points for each heat. Then judges add riders' heat scores together. **The rider with the most points wins.**

Riders soar into the air during a race.

# Gearing Up

Motocross racers wear jerseys. They also wear gear to protect themselves. Their pants have pads at the knees and thighs.

Riders wear gloves to protect their hands.

Helmets protect riders' heads. Goggles keep dirt from flying in their eyes. Chest protectors keep riders' torsos safe if they crash.

Motocross is split into groups or classes. Classes are based on engine sizes. Bikes with bigger engines have more power. But it's easier to control bikes with smaller engines.

# Tough Competition

The world's best Motocross racers compete at the X Games. The top rider wins a gold medal.

Mammoth Motocross started in 1968. Many future pros get their start at this amateur competition. Riders show off their skills and speed.

Riders compete at the 2021 FIM Motocross World Championship.

Racers make a turn at the 2021 Lucas Oil Pro Motocross Championship.

The Pro Motocross Championship challenges racers with tough courses. Obstacles such as turns and hills can slow racers down.

Tanya Muzinda has competed in the 65cc class. Classes are usually broken down by the rider's age or their bike's engine size.

Tanyaradzwa (Tanya) Muzinda of Zimbabwe became a Motocross champion at 15. She rode her first dirt bike when she was five.

Japanese racer Jo Shimoda has podium finishes in seven amateur championships. He also races Supercross—dirt bike racing in stadiums. It's a newer version of Motocross.

Jo Shimoda gives an interview after winning a race in 2021.

Dylan Ferrandis speeds up in the RedBud National in 2019.

In his first season as a Motocross racer, France's Dylan Ferrandis had a lot of highs and lows. He proved he was tough competition when he won the 2021 Pro Motocross Championship as a rookie.

Motocross demands a lot from its racers. They take on tough courses and high jumps. Fans love watching their favorite racers face off.

Fans will continue enjoying Motocross races!

# Bike Diagram

## Kawasaki KX450F

# How It Works

Builders make a lot of decisions when making dirt bikes. Most bikes are made from aluminum or steel. Aluminum is lighter, but steel lasts longer. Then builders decide what type of engine to use. The bigger the engine, the more power the bike has. Bikes with smaller engines are easier to handle. How would you build your dirt bike?

## Glossary

**amateur:** playing a sport without being paid

**class:** a group that competes against one another

**engine:** a machine that changes energy into mechanical motion

**heat:** one lap around a course

**obstacle:** something that riders must jump over on a course such as hills

**podium finish:** to finish within the top three spots

**pro:** short for professional, taking part in an activity to make money

**rookie:** a first-year competitor

**Supercross:** a type of dirt bike racing that takes place in stadiums

## Learn More

Britannica Kids: Motorcycle
https://kids.britannica.com/students/article/motorcycle/275952

Ducksters: MotoX Motocross
https://www.ducksters.com/sports/extrememotox.php

Golusky, Jackie. *Supercross: Rev It Up!* Minneapolis: Lerner Publications, 2023.

Hudak, Heather. *Motocross.* New York: AV2, 2021.

Lanier, Wendy Hinote. *Motocross.* Minneapolis: Pop!, 2021.

# Index



# Photo Acknowledgments

Image credits: Synto/Shutterstock, p. 4; MuratOzcelik/Shutterstock, p. 5; Todor Stoyanov/Shutterstock, p. 6; abu/Getty Images, p. 7; ako/Alamy Stock Photo, p. 8; AP Photo/Steve Lundy/Daily Herald, p. 9; AP Photo/Thurman James, pp. 10, 19; Nomad_Soul/Shutterstock, p. 11; AP Photo/Andrew Snook/Icon Sportswire, p. 12; Sean M. Haffey /Getty Images, p. 13; Gerard Spaans/BSR Agency/Getty Images, p. 14; AP Photo/Jeff Kardas, p. 15; Roberto Casimiro/Fotoarena/Alamy Stock Photo, p. 16; Thurman James/CSM/Alamy Stock Photo, p. 17; AP Photo/Michael Caterina, p. 18; Axl43/Pixabay CC0, p. 20.

Cover: Wolfgang Grebien/GEPA pictures/Sipa USA via AP.